A Year's
Journey

GEORGETTE C. DOAN

ARCHWAY
PUBLISHING

Archway Publishing books may be ordered
through booksellers or by contacting:

Archway Publishing
1663 Liberty Drive
Bloomington, IN 47403
www.archwaypublishing.com
1 (888) 242-5904

Because of the dynamic nature of the Internet, any web addresses or
links contained in this book may have changed since publication and
may no longer be valid. The views expressed in this work are solely those
of the author and do not necessarily reflect the views of the publisher,
and the publisher hereby disclaims any responsibility for them.

Any people depicted in stock imagery provided by Thinkstock are
models, and such images are being used for illustrative purposes only.
Certain stock imagery © Thinkstock.

ISBN: 978-1-4808-3785-0 (sc)
ISBN: 978-1-4808-3786-7 (e)

Library of Congress Control Number: 2016916304

Print information available on the last page.

Archway Publishing rev. date: 10/14/2016

Acknowledgments

I commend my parents' courage for raising ten children, giving us hope, and making our dreams a reality.

The courage and faith that my parents showed us through the years inspired this book. Just as Moses took his people to the land of milk and honey, my mom brought us to the best place on earth. When things looked bad and she wanted to give up, she would reach out to God. Replenished with faith and hope, she would try one more day and one more time. My parents are the solid posts in our lives; therefore the words *thank you* will never be enough.

Soon afterwards we got to California, as we were sitting around thanking God for all that He had done for us, we all thought that one of us should write the story of how we got there. The years have passed and no one has done it until now. Many thanks are extended to my family: Lisa, Cornel, Nicolina, Mike, Sandy, George, John, Lena, Augustin, Andrea, Violeta, Teodor, and Saveta.

Georgette C. Doan

Theme

For the most part, when you look at people or talk to someone, you don't think about their past. Was it hard or treacherous, or were they born with a silver spoon in their mouth? Raising ten children is hard work, but raising ten children in a communist country with very little opportunity is devastatingly difficult. My parents wanted our lives to be a little better than what our small country, Romania, offered. They took their lives and our future into their hands and left everything they owned behind—without regret. We had very little money, but because of our faith in God, we always had a roof over our heads and a hot meal.

I am sure you have heard all kinds of stories, funny and sad and all interesting in their own way. The story I am about to tell you is different from anything you have heard, and this one is true.

I will start by telling you a little about my family. My mom, Saveta, and my dad, Teodor, have ten children. Here they are from the oldest on down: Augustin, Lena, John, George, Sandy, Charlie (who is me, the storyteller), Mike, Zoe, Cornel, and Lisa. There are nineteen years between Augustin and Lisa. Violeta, Augustin's wife, also lived with us.

A series of events that would change my life began in April 1977. On a beautiful afternoon, our house burned down, and for the first time in our lives we had to rent a house. We lived in Timisoara, a large city in Romania. Until April 1977, we were happy in our own way.

I think it was spring break, because we were all home from school. Mom baked bread every Saturday in an outdoor brick oven that Dad had built. All the children were doing different things, and Mom had put the bread in to bake. It was an average day around the house. About six o'clock, a man pounded on our door, saying the roof was on fire. At that point, we all panicked and started to get water to put out the fire, but it was more than we could handle. We didn't have a phone and neither did any of our neighbors, but someone went to the nearest pay phone, which was a long walk away, to call the fire department.

All our neighbors helped us fight the fire and move our belongings out of the house. However, no one asked or checked to see if everyone had made it out of the house. In a short while, we realized that Lena had gone to take a nap in the back bedroom. As Sandy ran in to wake Lena, the window was bright with flames. As they were running out, the window exploded and the flames overtook the room.

About thirty minutes later, people from the fire department arrived. Later, as they were ready to leave, the chief was getting ready to give my dad a fine. He asked, "What kind of person are you to burn your house like this?"

Luckily, one of our neighbors, who was young and very pretty, talked the chief out of issuing a fine. The sun was going down, and we smaller kids were still crying. Our parents had a serious problem on their hands. I am sure they had faced problems before, but nothing like this.

About three blocks away from our burned-down house, one of our neighbors had just finished building a house. It was empty, so he let us stay in it for six weeks. We had insurance on our house, but it was not like the United States—we received no money for rebuilding. The insurance people told Dad that because he was a Christian, he should go to church and ask its people to help us. We had a small amount of money that the church gave us, but that was all.

Mom and Dad used all their savings to buy materials to rebuild. By the end of June, we had moved back into the half of the house that hadn't been damaged badly. Materials to finish the rebuilding were stacked in front of the house, but we had no money to hire people to do the work. Slowly the roof and kitchen were fixed, but the back bedrooms and walls were halfway up. Before the whole roof was done, Mom wanted to add a second story to the house. The ten children were growing, and Mom wanted all of us—married or not—to live with her, so she needed a big house. The second story started to go up. We made an assembly line to bring the bricks from the ground up to Dad, who was on a scaffold. Fairly soon, the walls took shape and started to look like a house again.

During the reconstruction, my parents were frustrated, especially Mom. We had no money and no help, and they were drowning in deep frustration. Mom said it was time to move on to make a better life for us kids. In the summer of 1977, they decided to apply for visas to move to the United States. After all that had happened they were ready to leave everything behind and never look back.

One evening, they told us about the visa application. We didn't understand much about it, but we were very happy. Mom said that it wasn't going to happen overnight, but a time would come when we would leave Romania and move to the United States.

After a few months, we asked Mom, "When are we going? Why is it taking so long?"

My parents are very religious people, and their response was, "Be patient. God will take care of us, and we will be safe wherever we go."

Dad would go to the office every few months and check on the visa application he had filed. The officials' response to my dad was always the same: "Go home. We will send you a response when we get to your forms." Life was getting worse for us day by day. Us kids, were starting to have serious doubts about leaving and finding a better life, but Mom always told us that we had to believe in God. He would provide a better way for us to live, she said, so we needed to be strong and not doubt Him.

At that time(1979) in Romania military service was mandatory and my brother John was due to enlist in the Romanian army. But Mom decided that he wasn't going to enlist, no matter what. The only way he could avoid enlistment was to leave the country, but we were still waiting for our visas, so that wasn't going to happen soon enough for him to avoid it.

In the summer of 1979, John tried to escape to Hungary, but unfortunately he was caught. About a month later, he again tried to cross the Hungarian border the same way. I have to say there is a God, because although John took the same route, hoping he would not be caught, he was caught by the same border patrol officer. John is very charming and can talk his way out of almost anything. The border patrol officer fed him and brought him home, but he didn't put John in jail, which was the way it usually went. The officer didn't even put handcuffs on him. Instead, he tied John's hands with a shoelace and told him if he really wanted to go, he should try the Yugoslavian border, because that was easier than the Hungarian border. John returned home, but his troubles were not over, because the military police were looking for him. But he was determined not to serve in the army.

In September, John left again—this time for the Yugoslavian border—and we didn't hear from him for a few weeks. When he had been caught on his two previous escape attempts, he had been back in a couple of days, but not this time. Mom became more and more worried, but at the same time she was happy, thinking that perhaps he had made it. The military police kept coming by every so often, looking for him.

At the beginning of November, we got a postcard from John. He was a free man in Austria, and Mom's tension dissipated. She was happy, and so were we. When the military policeman came the next time, Mom showed him John's card, so the officer never returned.

Augustin and Violeta had a daughter on October 20, 1979, which brought some happiness into our home. But winter was coming soon, and we were losing hope of getting an answer from the visa office. Life in general was getting harder day by day.

Early in 1980, we were hopeful that this was the year our lives would change, and it did—for the worse. For example, when we walked to the neighborhood store to buy simple items like milk and bread we had to wait in long lines. It seemed that every day the lines grew longer, supplies were more scarce, and the demand was higher. The word around town was that pretty soon we would be allowed to buy only a small, limited portion of groceries per family, and that a card was going to be issued to each family. This rumor scared us, so we started asking more often when we were going to leave all the madness behind. Mom always said, "Soon, honey, soon. Just believe that God will provide a way for us to start fresh in a better place."

Spring came and went pretty quickly. Our situation didn't change—there was still no news about our visa application. In April or so, Mom had a dream about us leaving, and she told us that the time for our move was getting closer. She dreamed that she was going somewhere, but in front of her was a tall, black, brick wall. She was trying to find a way around it, but the brick wall seemed to have no end. In her dream, a voice said, "Be patient. I will take it down so that you can go." In her dream, a hand reached down and pushed the wall away, but there were five more bricks in the way. She wanted to move the bricks, but the voice again said, "I am here to help you, and I will take them down for you." Then the hand reached for the last five bricks, and Mom woke up. After she told us about the dream, she seemed less frustrated and sad, because she knew that God was listening to her prayers.

Mom knew many people from all over the city, including people who commuted in from out of town. One woman in particular, Maria, lived far away from town, very close to Romania's border with Yugoslavia. Maria was a housekeeper in a restaurant and commuted to work six days a week. Mom and Maria were both Hungarian, and they became good friends.

Throughout the summer when Mom went grocery shopping, she made her way by the restaurant just to say hi and talk about kids and life in general. Each time they saw each other, Mom hinted to Maria about where she lived and how close it was to the border. Maria knew Mom was interested in leaving but didn't know how many people were going to go at once. She said the time had to be right, because many military police officers and workers maintained the cornfields between her home and the border. Beyond that, she said, there were a lot of traps; it was as if the area were an obstacle course.

Then it was September again, and we kids were back in school. I was in school Monday through Saturday, and a couple of weeks down the line I came home one Saturday and told Mom I had had a very weird dream. She said, "Tell me what it was about." I told her that I had been at school and she had come on Tuesday night at ten o'clock at night and insisted that I get ready to go home. I was telling her it was Tuesday night, and I didn't go home until Saturday. In the dream, she said, "We are leaving right now no matter what day it is."

I usually went to school a week at a time because it was a boarding school. I realized that I hadn't seen George for a couple of weeks, and Mom said he had gone to Maria's house and was trying to escape. She was not sure whether he had made it, because he had been gone from Maria's house for a week. Maria's son Karol was the same age as George, and he was gone, too. It was very hard to find out if they had made it or not. They could have been caught and thrown in jail, or they could have made it and just not been able to send postcards home yet. Mom and Maria were extremely scared and worried about their boys.

On Friday, October 24, we finished our homework and got permission from our teacher to go to the movies. As I walked backward toward the school's front gate, one of my friends said: "Why is your mother coming to see you today?"

I said, "No, she's not coming today."

"I saw her check in at the gate," he said.

I started to walk faster and saw her. As I hugged her, she whispered in my ear, "We are going to America on Tuesday." I stepped back and couldn't speak. Everyone was looking at me.

My lips were moving, but no words came out of my mouth. I was trying very hard to say, "What changed all of a sudden in one week?"

My friends left to go to the movies, and I stayed visiting with my mom. She said, "Do you remember your dream? Tuesday is the day, but you can't tell anyone. When you come home tomorrow, be sure to bring your tennis shoes and your P.E. clothes." She gave me a bag of candy and said, "I have to go." She had stayed about twenty minutes total.

As I walked away from the gate, some of my friends who hadn't gone to the movies asked why she had come and why she had left so soon. I made up some lie that she was going to visit someone in the area. I had a knot in my stomach through that whole night but tried very hard not to show it.

My mind was gone. That night I packed my few things to take home as usual, but I looked at them and wanted to give them away. I gave a few items to my closest friends. It was finally nine o'clock: lights out. I didn't have to hide my happiness any longer, but at the same time I couldn't sleep. My mind was a million miles away.

Saturday came, and I knew I had a long day ahead. As soon as I saw my teacher, I asked for permission to leave at one o'clock that afternoon, which was normal for me, but she said no. I cleaned my desk and locker and put things away neatly, watching the hands on the clock. I looked around to be sure no one saw me looking at the clock constantly. At noon or so, my teacher came over and said, "I know you want to go, but you have to attend a student body meeting. Then you can go home." The day got to be longer and longer. Everyone was talking and acting as if they were in slow motion, and I was the only one who knew or saw it. If I wasn't looking at the clock, I was looking at my bag, wondering how much more waiting I could take. It was killing me inside.

The student body meeting started at four thirty. By then I was looking at the second hand on the clock, but it wasn't moving fast enough. Finally six o'clock came and I could go. I didn't have to change because I had been ready since one o'clock. Slowly I got my bag and said goodbye to some kids because I knew I wasn't going to see them again. In my mind I was running to the front gate, but in actuality I walked very slowly and looked around for the last time. As I walked to the bus stop, I heard my name being called. I tried hard to ignore it, but the voice kept calling, and I realized it was my best friend, Mihaela. I didn't want to talk to her on the bus, but she kept insisting on knowing what was wrong with me. I was afraid that because she was my best friend, I would tell her what I was doing. I didn't want to get her in trouble, which I knew she would if I told her. After we got off the bus, we said our goodbyes, and she went her way and I went mine. Then I had the biggest smile on my face all the way home. I didn't have to hide my happiness anymore.

When I got home, it was dark and everyone was home. Everyone was kind of busy, because Dad and Grandpa had butchered a pig early in the morning that still required a little cleaning. I wanted to ask Mom how we were going to go, or something about our leaving, but I didn't know how to approach her, because no one was acting any differently.

I looked around and didn't see our dogs or cats, so I asked about them. We had two dogs. The big one was Rita, and the little mutt was Puffy. The cats didn't have any particular name. Mom said that Rita had died by the boat on the dock where she had spent a lot of time with my brothers, and Puffy was very sick and probably wouldn't make it through the night. We had had our cats for a few years, and they had never run away, but they had last been seen a week or so earlier and hadn't come back. They buried Rita by the river because she was always playing tag with my brothers from the boat to the water, back and forth all summer long.

The next morning Mom called Puffy to see how he was, but there was no answer. She went outdoors to the brick oven where he usually slept, and he was dead. The night before, Mom had made a bed for him in the house. He loved his outdoor bed by the brick oven, which was always warm. He must have crept out of the house during the night. Mom said our animals left us instead of us leaving them. In a way, I think she was happy because we had talked about who would take care of them.

The day went by slowly. Mom did some laundry and put things in certain bags set aside in the closet. On Sunday night she told us about the journey we were about to take. Dad worked on Sunday and had Monday off. Lena, Augustin, and Violeta didn't go to work on Monday, and none of us kids went to school. We kept a low profile so our neighbors wouldn't notice any change.

Lena, Sandy, and Zoe were supposed to go to Maria's house on Monday night. Mom sent a propane tank with the girls as an excuse to go there. Propane tanks were a precious commodity to have in a home. In town a few guys started to harass the girls and tried to steal the propane tank. The girls didn't get to Maria's house but had to turn around and go back home. After the girls returned, we sat and talked about what was going to happen on Tuesday. We checked our bags to be sure we had everything we needed. Each bag had underclothing, pants, shirts, a sweater, a pair of shoes, and socks. It was very important to have small bags because they wouldn't be so heavy.

Mom and Dad put together small groups to leave from the house. Before we went to bed, the alarm was set for 4:30 a.m. for the first group to get ready to go on the morning of October 28, 1980. Augustin, Violeta, and Andrea were one group, and Lena, Sandy, and Zoe were another. When the alarm went off, we all got up and felt anxiety setting in. Augustin, Violeta, and Andrea were ready to go, so the three of them walked to the bus stop. A few minutes later, Lena, Sandy, and Zoe walked to the same bus stop, which was very close to our house. We were very quiet so we could hear the bus coming. About five minutes later the girls walked out, we heard the bus. We were pretty sure they had all boarded the same bus, but they were to sit separately and not talk to one another until they got to Maria's house. They took separate commuter trains so they wouldn't be together. After the girls left, Mom got down on her knees and prayed for all of them and Maria to be safe.

Around 8:00 a.m. Dad, Mike, and Cornel were ready to go. Now the sun was out, and it wasn't as cold. Dad took each son by the hand and started walking down to the bus stop. Again, we waited to hear the bus come and go, and Mom prayed again. There was a lot of praying and a lot of commotion that morning.

Then it was only me, Mom, and Lisa left at home. Mom and I started to clean up, make beds, and put things away. It was quiet, but Mom started to hum and sing church songs. Around 9:30 a.m. or so, my dad's cousin, Marion, came over. Mom and Cousin Marion started talking, reading the Bible, and praying. Lisa and I were playing around. As I put things away and cleaned a little, I found a lot of loose change. Lisa had this big jar of change, and before we left, the jar was filled up. I looked at everything for the last time. Deep down I was sure that I wasn't going to see our home again anytime soon.

We were ready to leave, but Mom was waiting for a cousin of ours to stay in the house for a few days so no one would think it had been left empty. Around 11:00 a.m., Cousin Alan came, and Mom said, "We will be gone for a few days." She told him we were going to Bucuresti to see why our visa papers were taking so long.

Nothing about this statement or our actions was unusual; a lot of people were doing just that. Cousin Alan did not ask many questions. He just said, "I will see you when you get back." As Mom talked with Alan, I looked at the house and front yard, wondering if the bulbs would ever come up next year. We said our goodbyes and started to go toward the bus stop.

Cousin Marion walked to the corner while holding in her tears. At the corner she gave me and Lisa a hug and told us to be good and listen to our mom. She walked straight ahead, and we turned right. I asked Mom if she knew the truth, and Mom said she was the only person who did— no one else. As we started walking to the bus stop, Mom said, "I hope the bus will get here soon." We got to the station, and about two minutes later, we could see the bus at the corner.

In every neighborhood there's one busybody who annoys everyone and talks your ear off if you let him or her. This woman liked my mom because Mom never stopped her from talking and never walked away from her, which some people had done. As we got on the bus, she showed up and got on. We walked all the way to the back and sat down. Mom whispered to me as we sat down, "If she comes and sits near us, just let me talk to her." Lisa was asking silly questions and just being a kid, and Mom was happy to be talking to her. The old lady saw us sitting in the back and waved to us, but didn't come near us or talk to us at all.

Before we knew it, our stop had come, and we were ready to get off. Mom was relieved that the old woman had left us alone. It was very unusual for her not to say a word to Mom. We crossed the street and took the No. 2 cable car that would take us all the way to the train station. Once on the cable car, we sat down. Mom held Lisa on her lap, and I sat by the window. It was a long ride, but none of us said very much, so it was a quiet ride. Mom looked around to see if she recognized anyone, and every so often she whispered, "Thank God."

At the train station, we sat on a bench while Mom got the train tickets. As we waited, Mom leaned over and said, "If anyone asks us where we are going, just tell them we are going to visit Grandma."

There were three trains that we were supposed to take. The first two trains were regular, everyday trains on which people didn't care who was riding. When we got off the second train, we waited for the small commuter train. It was not much of a station, small and not very crowded at this time of day. It must have been two thirty or so in the afternoon. In this part of the country in small towns, everyone knew everyone and measured each other up, wondering whether they were from out of town. No one was talking, but one old man had a packet full of loose change and was walking up and down the small pathway. After a while he got to be pretty annoying. Everyone looked at him, but no one said a word. To pass the time, I started to count how many times he walked by us. By the time the train had arrived, I think I had gotten to fifty or so.

We got on the train and sat down. Lisa and I sat across from each other by the window, and Mom sat next to Lisa. There were a lot of military police officers on the train, walking up and down and looking at everyone but not saying much. The conductor came by to see our tickets. Mom gave them to him, and while he checked them, he asked Lisa where she was going. She said, "I am going to see my grandma." He handed the tickets back to Mom, and a few minutes later, a military policeman came and asked Mom why we were traveling so far out of town. Mom said there was corn to be picked and that Grandma needed help because she couldn't do it by herself.

Soon after, we got off and started walking to Maria's house, which wasn't very far from the station. We walked through her front gate, she opened the front door and we went inside. Mom gave her a big hug and talked to her in Hungarian. Dad joined in the conversation. We were the last ones to get there, and everyone was sitting around in the front room. All the curtains were closed and the house was a little dark, but it was for our protection. I looked up at the clock on the wall, and it was close to four. Mom was relieved that we had all made it to Maria's safely.

Augustin and Violeta were in her backyard helping to pick Maria's corn. Maria's house was not very big. She had four rooms, including the kitchen. We all sat around not doing very much of anything. I was quiet. It must have been four thirty or so when we heard a loud knock at the front gate. Instantly, we all thought that this was the end. We were scared to death. Maria looked out the kitchen window, and her face dropped. Without any words, we all hid in the back two bedrooms, under the beds, in the closet, or anyplace we found. We heard a man's footsteps in the kitchen pacing up and down.

The man, a military policeman, said, "I hear that you have some visitors."

Maria replied, "Yes, my grandchildren came to help me with the picking of the corn."

"Where are they now?"

"They are in the back picking corn," Maria said.

"By the way, where is that son of yours?"

"He is gone with his friend in town for a while."

"What are you doing in the house?" the military policeman asked.

"I just came in to start dinner and am putting some tea on. Would you like some?" she offered.

The military policeman said, "Oh, no. You're doing okay then? I'll go now."

Maria replied, "Thanks for coming by."

He left and walked up and down on the sidewalk a couple of times before leaving. A few minutes later, Maria came and said we could come out. She said he must have seen something or someone who didn't live in this area. After this scary ordeal, Mom had us children take a nap. She said, "Rest for two hours so you kids won't be tired later." When we woke up, it was dark out, about seven thirty or eight at night, and the lights in the kitchen were low. The curtains were closed, and Mom said we couldn't walk around too much because it would make figures in the window. Maria lived by herself at this time. Her son had been gone with George since September.

Mom and Maria had fixed a light dinner, and we ate without talking much. As we sat around drinking tea, Maria said the last train came into town a little after nine o'clock and everyone was off the street by nine thirty or so. She also said that once all the people were at home, they didn't go out or care who else was out; however, military policemen were out patrolling the streets. The problem was trying to go out without letting the military police officers see us.

We all took turns going to the bathroom and got our bags out of the closet. Once we were all done, we sat around in the front room in a circle, and Dad read from the Bible. We all got down on our knees and prayed, including Maria. Andrea was still sleeping because she had a bit of a cold, and Mom and Violeta had given her some cough medicine. Mom tied a sheet in a triangle around her somehow and held Andrea in it. Soon after that, we said goodbye to Maria and started to walk out the door. The last thing Maria said was, "Just walk straight, and you will be okay—God be with you all."

Till then Mom's plan had worked out pretty well, but from then on, we needed help from up above from our dear God. As we walked down a narrow, dark street, no noise came from anywhere, not even barking dogs, and that had been a big fear—that dogs would bark and people would come out and see us. Soon after, the sidewalk stopped, and we walked on a dirt road past the cemetery. Mom whispered that pretty soon we would get to the cornfields and no one would see us then. When we got to the cornfields, the corn had been cut and the fields were empty. Only the stubs from the cornstalks stood about eighteen inches from the ground. We had to be careful not to trip and fall. As we walked through the empty field, the moon got bigger and brighter, which was good in one way because we could see, and at the same time was bad because others could see us. At this point, however, there was no turning back.

We had walked for a good stretch when Cornel said, "Mom, there is a shiny thing lying on the ground up there." When we got to it, Dad barely touched it, and we all stepped carefully over it. We knew all kinds of traps were in the fields, and this was the first one we spotted. It was a very thin wire about twelve inches off the ground. If we had stepped on or tripped across it, it would have sent signals up into the air like fireworks, with a loud noise and bright colors.

The moon seemed to get bigger and brighter like a big lightbulb in the sky. We had just gotten over the anxiety from the wire when we saw a ditch ahead. We slowly walked up to it. Once we were all near it, we looked at it for a second or two and started one by one to go across. The ditch itself was wide and shallow, and although it had about two feet of water in it, it wasn't too bad. Augustin went first, and as he went up on the other side, he said, "On this side, there is a wire lying along the ground." He sat and made sure no one accidentally stepped on or touched it. We had just recovered from one episode and then walked into another, but we kept a calm frame of mind.

We all knew it wasn't going to be easy. Mom was talking to us all along, calming us, no matter what. As we walked along and whispered to one another, someone said, "I think I hear people's voices."

Mom said, "Maybe other people are escaping like we are." We looked around to see where the voices were coming from. Because the moon was so big and bright, we could see a man walking to the far right of us. We heard voices coming from the left and saw another man. At this point, we were all scared, to say the least. They were walking toward each other. One of them had a radio that he had turned up loudly, and both of them had flashlights, with which they were playing tag. The two of them talked to each other on CB radios.

At that point, we thought it was the end: we were caught. We all sat down and were sure they were walking over to us. They were only about two hundred feet in front of us, and we just waited to see what was going to happen. They met each other and talked and laughed, still playing with the flashlights. After they had talked for a couple of minutes or so, one of them started to walk back to his post, and then the other did as well. After we watched this exchange of posts, we sat thanking God for looking out for us. We waited several minutes after they left, and then slowly got up and started to walk again.

I can't tell you how relieved we all were. There are no words for that, but as we walked, the moon hit just so on a very shiny line—so brightly that we could all see it from a few yards away. After we walked over to it carefully, and about six feet or so away was a deep, wide ditch with a tall fence on the other side. We looked down at the water in the ditch, but there was no way of knowing how deep it was. Dad and Augustin went first. Dad stood on the other side of the ditch, and then Lena went down. She and Augustin stood in the water and carried each one of us over so we wouldn't get wet.

Mom, Dad, Lena, and Augustin were wet from the waist down. On the other side, we waited for Dad to make a hole in the fence.

There were a lot of tin cans hanging on the fence and fence posts to make noise if anyone tried to climb over it. As Dad looked for a spot to go through, we took the cans off the fence gently so there wouldn't be any noise for us or anyone else who came. He was about to lift the chain-link fence when he discovered that it was already cut and just hooked back up, barely hanging. We all went through a hole that was about two feet off the ground and a couple of feet wide. As we passed on to the other side of the fence, we took some more cans off and closed the gap.

On this side of the fence, the grass was high, up to our waists or better. It was hard to tell if we had crossed the border because we thought that a strip of land marked it, but there was no land, and at the same time, it was different from before. There hadn't been weeds before, but now we were in an empty field with tall weeds.

We still had to walk, so it didn't make much difference where the border was. It was a little hard to see what was ahead of us, so we had to be even more careful about where we stepped. After walking for a few minutes, we saw grass moving not far up in front of us, but there was no wind. We all stopped and waited to see what or who was going to pop up from the grass. We sat for a couple of minutes, watching the rippling coming slowly toward us. We got scared again. The couple of minutes seemed very long, but suddenly two birds flew up from the grass. Slowly we got up from the ground, one by one, looking around to be sure it was safe to go again.

We walked through this tall grass, not knowing whether we were still in Romania or in Yugoslavia. After about an hour of walking, we came to a wide strip of clear land, about six feet wide and long from side to side. We all made sure to leave our footprints to let them know that we were many in a group of all ages, big and small, young and old.

Now was the moment of truth. We had crossed the border for sure, and stopped for a minute to regroup. Until then we had walked straight just like Maria had said. Mom and Dad looked around, and we planned where to go and how to get away from the border that we had crossed just yards away. There were only empty fields ahead of us, but far, far away on the right side of us was a lighthouse. We started to walk toward it. After a good while, we started to see weeds and trees and thought that on the other side of the trees, there would be a town or some houses where we could get some help. The weeds were getting taller, and we started going uphill.

After a short while, the ground sloped down and had water in it. It looked like a swamp or a marsh, but we thought that if we got past the trees, we would be all right. The trees were getting closer and closer, but the water was getting deeper. We were determined to get to the trees, but when the water was to our waists and getting deeper, Mom and Dad told us to go back and walk around the marsh, still keeping the lighthouse in sight.

We got out of the water. Until then, no one had complained about anything, but now we smaller kids were getting cold and asked if we could stop. Mom said, "Soon enough, we will, so we can all change from these wet clothes." Mom, Dad, Lena, and Augustin had been wet for a much longer time than the rest of us, but we were small and couldn't take it as well as they did. We got back to the fields and walked toward the lighthouse until we finally stopped to change clothes right in the empty fields. We all got our change of clothes from our bags that we had been so careful not to get wet, and left all our wet clothes right there. We changed everything down to our shoes.

As we changed, we wondered what time it was. Dad said it was 3:00 a.m., and because we were getting warmer, we started to talk out loud and make conversation. Someone said, "What a way to start on a Wednesday." It was October 29, 1980. What a way to start a day! The smaller children began to complain that they were getting tired, but Mom said we should walk some more to get closer to the lighthouse and perhaps closer to a small town so we could get help. To the left, the corn hadn't been picked yet, and there were tractor tire tracks in front. Mom said this was surely the way to get to town. Lisa was getting sleepy and wanted to stop for a short time, but Mom wanted us to walk until dawn. As we walked on the tractor road, there were puddles here and there, and at times we would step in them. There were a lot of tumbleweeds along the road. All of our clean pants and shoes were full of mud and weeds.

Mike and Cornel asked Mom if, when daylight came, the wing above us would go away. Mom asked them, "What wing? What are the two of you talking about?"

They said they were referring to the big, white wing that had been with us since we had been on the road the previous night. Mike said, "I've been looking at it all night long and was wondering if we would still see it in the daylight."

"I knew God would be with us," Mom said, and thanked God again for His presence.

As we walked, our conversation was slowing because we were all sleepy. I remember after a while just moving my feet without having my eyes open, waking up every time I stepped into a puddle. It got to be just a little light, and Mom said there were some houses up ahead and we would stop soon.

At this point my eyes just barely saw someone else's feet moving in front of me, and I followed along. I was just listening to whomever was talking, but there wasn't much of conversation. Dad saw some rocks and said they would be a good place to rest. The sun was rising here and there, and we could see people starting to walk on the road. We were very close to town. I remember taking a napkin out of my jacket pocket, placing it on one of the rocks, and sitting on it. Mike was near me, resting on the same rock, and asked why I had put the napkin down, because I was already covered with mud and weeds. We both laughed and started to wake ourselves up.

I think we sat there for thirty minutes or so. Before walking again, we tried to clean off the mud and tumbleweeds. We did a fair job. We woke Andrea up, and now Violeta was holding her. This was the first time Andrea had woken up. Mom had carried her all night long. We got very close to the town's streets. People were going every which way. It must have been somewhere close to 7:00 a.m. Dad and Augustin walked in front and asked some people where we could find the police station. As we got to the street, people stared at us. They had reason to, because we were muddy and there were a lot of us, big and small.

We hadn't gone too far before we walked into a building with two big double doors at the entrance. We all walked in and were shown to two other doors. We were told to sit down in a big conference room with a long table at one side with a long bench along the window. One by one we sat down on the bench. Two men came in and showed us to a washroom, where we were able to clean our hands and shoes. We tried very hard not to look messy, but pulling the tumbleweeds from our pants ruined the material, so we looked ragged. As we came back to the bench, the two men paced up and down from the room to the hallway, talking. As we warmed up at the heater, which was alongside the bench, we didn't all fit side by side. The two men asked some of us to sit in the hallway where there was another bench next to a heater.

At this point, we all realized that we were not in Romania anymore, because we couldn't understand what the men were saying. We all talked about what we had imagined in our minds, but this was the real thing—no dream, no imagination, but the real thing. As I thought about all of this, the two men came in and brought us bread, salami, and tea, and milk for Andrea. We didn't eat very much because we were more sleepy than anything. The two men talked quite a bit on the phone. Between 10:30 and 11:00 a.m. the two of them paced even more, looking out the window. The sun was bright, and it looked nice outside. One of them opened a side door leading out and gestured for us to get up and go. The only thing he said to us was, "Let's go," so we walked out.

Outside sat two white vans with the back doors open. They told us to get into the vans. Mom didn't want us to be separated, but we had no choice, so we had to go in separate vans. Mom and five of the smaller kids, including me, got into one van, and the rest got into the other one. We heard the doors close on the other van, and within seconds our doors were closed too. Our van had two benches on each side and no windows. The area between the driver and us was closed, and the back door had a little grid that allowed just a bit of light to come through. We were in the dark otherwise. After a few minutes, we were able to see one another and just a little bit outside. We asked Mom where we were going, but she didn't know. After a few minutes, we were going pretty fast and the road seemed bumpy. Mom said she hoped they weren't taking us back, because she had heard that sometimes they drove you back to the Romanian border and just handed you over to the border patrol.

As we sat in darkness, wondering where we were going, the van came to a stop. The other van stopped too, and the two drivers spoke to each other: the other van needed gas. We couldn't see anything; we could just hear what was going on.

After a few minutes, the back door opened and one of the drivers handed Mom a big chocolate bar. He smiled at us as he closed the door. We sat very quietly, listening to hear if the other van was coming along. Soon after, we were on the same bumpy road. We must have been on the road about an hour when the van stopped again. It was backed up to the front door of a four-story building, as was the other van. The doors opened, and the man motioned for us to get out, so we did. As we walked slowly to the front door of the building, a lot of people outside stared at us.

We followed the man who had driven us down a long, narrow hallway. On each side of the hallway, there must have been eight to ten doors, and at each door, people were looking at us. We were shown to the end of the hallway to a big room on our right with a bench running along the wall on two sides. We sat down one by one. I looked at this room. It had light green tiles all around, and in one corner was a shower with the curtain partially closed. We could still see above and below the curtain. Blood was splattered all over the walls behind the curtain. I sat next to Mike, wondering if we were going to be next. At the same time we joked about it just to keep ourselves awake. Mike had his head on my shoulder, and I was leaning on him. Every few minutes, we fell asleep, but the two men who had taken us there kept coming in. They wanted to talk to Mom or Dad and would take them down the hall to do so.

After an hour or more, we were asked to stand and walk back outside, where we got into a van. Mom, Dad, Lena, and Augustin stayed behind and said that we would go somewhere for two or three days and then they would join us. Violeta was the grown-up with us kids. We got into the white van and were driven across town. It was a regular van with windows and comfortable seats. We crossed a small, white brick bridge, and in front of it was a large house with many levels. The van slowed down, and someone opened the gate in front. We drove in and got out. No one in the house spoke Romanian, so we couldn't understand them and they couldn't understand us. We were shown to a small room with beds in it. We were told to go to sleep, which was all we wanted to do. Later we were awakened by a woman who told us to go and eat. It was dark outside and we heard a lot of talking, but there was no one in the dining room.

Somehow we knew that this place was an orphanage and that the kids were getting ready for bed. When we had arrived earlier, the kids had been at school while we slept. The woman was very nice. She sat us down and gave us dinner and tried to talk to us. She asked us where we were from, and we told her. She left for a minute, and when she came back, she brought a boy named Ben who spoke Romanian. We sat at the table for a while and talked to them. We were happy to have someone who could talk to us. We stayed in the dining room and talked until 9:00 p.m. or so. The dining room was very clean and had round tables with red-and-white-checked tablecloths—very homey. Ben walked us around to show us where the washrooms were and said that if we needed anything, he would get it for us. We were just grateful to be there. It was still Wednesday—what a day! After 10:00 p.m. we went back to sleep.

Early Thursday morning, a handful of boys ran into our room and dragged Mike and Cornel out of bed, saying something, and a few minutes later we saw them watching TV with a lot of the other boys. All morning long, several kids opened the door to our room and then ran away. Ben came before he went to school. We asked him why everyone kept coming in to look at us and then run away. Ben said the boys had never seen anyone who wasn't Yugoslavian, and were curious about us.

The home was only for boys. We stayed there until Saturday. In the meantime, we adjusted well, and Ben spent all of his free time with us.

He liked Zoe a lot, and when we left on Saturday, he was crying, wanting to go with us. We wanted to take him with us, but we had no authority in that situation. Ben was about fourteen years old. Mom and the rest would not have minded at all. Mom probably would have said, "The more, the merrier."

When the van came back for us on Saturday, we all walked down to it. Ben said he had been there a long time, but this was the only time he had felt like he was part of a family. We all gave him a hug before we got in the van, and as the van started to go, Ben was left behind, waving. We knew he sat there for a long time, because we watched him until the van made a turn.

We were back to riding without knowing where we were going. The only thing Ben had told us was that they were going to take us to Mom and the rest of our family. We were in the van for about forty-five minutes and heading out of town. The van stopped in front of a hotel, and we all got out and walked into the lobby and sat on the couches while the driver talked to the clerk at the counter. After a few minutes, another van stopped, and when the door opened, Mom, Dad, Lena, and Augustin got out. We hugged, glad to see everyone. The two men drivers asked us how many rooms we wanted. One man had four keys in his hand, and Mom said three would be fine. The two men had us follow them down a hallway. They opened the doors to three rooms and said, "You will stay here for a while." They showed us where the dining room was and told us to go eat there three times a day. Someone would come and start our paperwork to go wherever we wanted to go. Before the men left, they said, "There is one thing you must keep in mind at all times: none of you should talk to anyone, and if anyone starts talking to you, walk away."

Sunday was our first day together in a new country. We walked outside on the premises of the hotel, which was for truckers who passed through the country in their big Mack trucks and eighteen-wheelers. It was very close to the freeway on the outside of town. All the waiters at the restaurant spoke English and their own language, but not a bit of Romanian. We had a table where we sat at each meal. It was a nice place with nice people.

On Monday we were picked up and shown how to get to an office where a lot of questions were asked and paperwork was completed. The office was downtown quite a ways from where we were staying. We all sat in the waiting room, and after a few minutes, a woman named Olga came and greeted us in Romanian and asked us to go into her office. She said, "Before we start anything, I have to tell you that from now on, you shouldn't all come to every meeting. It's not necessary. And one more thing that's very important: when you come, never talk to anyone, even in this office. You will hear and see a lot of Romanian people come through, but don't give in. The only person who will handle your case is me and only me, so don't discuss your case with anyone else in the office."

Dad asked her why and she said she had heard a lot of rumors that many people were looking for us. Romanian government personnel were very curious and wanted to know how such a large group of people had crossed the border without being seen by the police or them knowing anything about it. "They would love to have you back, and always have spies at the most unusual times and places. Now, if you want to go back, you do whatever you want, but if you want to be safe, follow these instructions."

At the second visit, Olga talked Dad into going to Australia instead of America, because they had a straight contract with Australia. If we really wanted to go to America, she said, we would have to go to Austria, because that's where the refugee camp was. Dad talked to us about it, and it sounded pretty good. He brought back a lot of brochures about Australia. All the pictures made it look like a good place to grow up, so we were all sold on going to Australia.

At the beginning of November, the woman at the office said that within six to eight weeks we would be in our new location, where we would stay for good. Our appointments at the office were scheduled for a time when no one else was there. It snowed a lot of the time in November. We kids often went to the side of the hotel to play in the snow. They had a large open area with evergreen trees. It looked really nice with the snow on the ground and all over the trees. We seldom went into town. Everywhere we went, we traveled on foot and kept to ourselves. Dad was at the office once a week with the hope that he would return with good news.

Before Christmas we had an appointment at the Australian Embassy, all of us together. The staff there saw us but didn't say much to us.

We were very excited that soon we would board Quantas Airlines. We had seen pictures of a big, white airplane with a kangaroo on the tail. after we were sent for medical evaluations, which made us think it would all be happening soon.

Christmas came and went with not much going on. We waited for it to pass so we would get our answer. Dad went to the office, and when he came back, he told us that although the embassy wanted us to go, they wanted the young family— Augustin, Violeta, Andrea, and Lena—to go first. They assured us that the rest of us would follow soon after. Mom didn't like that they were splitting up our family, but at the same time, she was told it would be for a very short period of time. Lena refused to go until all of us could.

In the middle of January, Augustin, Violeta and Andrea left to go to Sydney, Australia. We were told that because there were six kids and Lena, it was a little hard to find a sponsor for such a large family. So we had to be patient a little longer. There wasn't much to do at the hotel. Lena and Sandy bought some thread to make some macramé projects. The two of them invented a whole new way to make it because they didn't have the proper needle. Mom let us play out in the snow from time to time, but we stayed in 90 percent of the time. We had a Romanian/English dictionary from somewhere and tried to learn English from it, but we didn't know how to pronounce the words or how to make short sentences. It became very frustrating.

After a while we started to have fun with it, and it became our way of entertaining ourselves. We would have gone bonkers with nothing to do and no answer, just waiting. Time went by very slowly. In February we were told that the embassy staff wanted to see us again. We were very happy because we figured we were on our way, too. We had received a card from Augustin and Violeta, and they were doing well. Mom was happy to hear from them. After we went to the embassy, the officials took a long time to let us know one way or the other. To make the time pass, we walked in the fields where no one could see us. It was a way to get away from thinking "what if" or "what if not." We spent lots of afternoons picking small wild black plums.

One late February day, we went to the office. At that time we were told that the Australian government thought Mom and Dad were too old and we were too young, so we couldn't go to Australia. Now Olga couldn't help us any longer, and we had to think of Plan B. Plan B was to go to Austria and have them help us go to America. But there was a problem with that, because we didn't have any passports or money. Olga said they would provide train tickets and a letter for us to give to the Yugoslavian border patrol agents, but when it came to the Austrian patrol, we would be on our own. If anyone asked us about where we stayed or where we had come from, we couldn't say anything that had to do with that office.

On Monday, March 2, Dad went to the office by himself and returned just before lunch. Olga had given him the train tickets, letter, and two bags of canned food for the road and wished us luck. After lunch two men came, checked us out of the hotel, and told us which bus went to the train station. The two men left, and we went to our rooms and got our few things together. Soon after we left. Our train tickets were from Beograd to Gratz, which was the first big city in Austria. About 5:00 p.m., we got to the train station where our train was due to arrive. As we waited, Dad went to buy bread and some bottled water.

The train pulled in, and we all got on in one compartment. We were in a hurry for the train to start going, but it sat in the station for a while. Night was coming fast. The train finally pulled away from the platform. Soon after, the controller came and knocked at the door to ask for our tickets. Dad handed him our tickets, and he looked at us and smiled, punched a hole in the tickets, handed them back to Dad, and left. The train stopped a couple of times, but the conductor didn't ask for the tickets. He just looked and smiled. It was pretty late by the time we ate and a new controller came and asked Dad for the tickets again. Throughout the night, he came and punched another hole in the tickets. We slept off and on through the night. In the morning the controller walked up and down, telling everyone to get out their passports—the next stop was Austria.

The train slowed down and pulled into the station. We heard a lot of commotion with people getting on and off the train. Then we heard, "Passports, passports." It became very scary. Men dressed in uniforms knocked at doors. The voices were getting closer, and we turned into stones. We knew our turn was coming. A loud knock at our door came, and the man said, "Passports, please." Dad asked him if he was Yugoslavian and he said yes, so Dad handed him the letter. He opened it and then said, "Passports, please," but Dad just pointed to the letter. He turned to his partner and they talked to each other for a few minutes. He looked at us again and folded the letter, put it in his coat pocket, and walked away.

That was the easy part of this whole thing. Two things could happen next: one, they would knock on the door and find out we didn't have passports and throw us off the train; or two, they could skip our door, which would have been good. As the voices were next door, we prayed for a miracle to happen. One of the men knocked at the door with his baton and said, "Passports, please," and Dad said in Romanian, "We gave them to the other man." He looked at us and turned to ask his partner, who just passed him by to go to the next compartment.

In the next compartment, there was a lot of noise from bottles clinking. We knew they had very strict laws about transporting alcohol and tobacco over country borders. We sat very quietly, listening to what was going on in the next compartment. At the same time, we were scared to death. We could hear the two men's voices and the other people as well as lots of bottles being moved around. Suddenly it was quiet, and we knew that it was our turn and that it could be the end of us. We all sat motionless and waited. I don't think we even breathed. It got quieter and quieter and no one came.

Suddenly, the train started to move. There was no whistle signal, only the wave of a flag. We all broke out in a sigh of relief. The train moved faster and faster. The controller came by, and we showed him the tickets. He didn't say anything else. Then we all took turns going to the bathroom. We came back to our seats and thanked God for being with us and watching over us in our time of need. As we all stopped shaking from that experience, the train started slowing down and we saw the sign for Gratz, where our ride was over. We got our luggage and headed for the door.

It was Tuesday, March 3, a sunny morning, and the train station was not very crowded. We noticed that it was the cleanest place we had seen so far. As we walked, we asked a man where the police station was, but he gave us a long look and walked away. We just walked down the street looking around and finally saw a police car. We asked another man where the police station was, and he pointed down the street. We all walked in and began telling them in our own way where we wanted to go, and suddenly a lot of them came around, trying to figure us out.

They took us into a side room and got someone who spoke Romanian to ask us how we had gotten as far as we had without anyone stopping us along the way. We told them everything except about the office in Yugoslavia. They kept going in and out of the room. Somehow we got through to them that we wanted to go the refugee camp in

Traiskirchen. They told us that they usually had a bus that took refugees like us to Traiskirchen once a week, on Fridays, so we had to wait until then. We didn't have anywhere to stay and it was only Tuesday, so they took us to the county jail and said we had to wait there until Friday.

We were taken to the county jail in a van, and like before, there was a lot of staring when we got there. We walked up to the second floor, and the man who was with us opened a big, metal door with a small window and a slot beneath that. He explained to us that our food would come through the slot and that in thirty minutes, we should give the containers back. We would get three meals a day. The room was big and long and had thirteen beds lined along the two walls. In the other corner was a toilet with a sink next to it. In the middle of the room a wooden table sat with all kinds of names etched in the tops, sides, and legs. The windows were small and very high off the ground.

Meanwhile, the police investigated to see if we were who we said we were. We waited for Friday, but the days stood still for us. On Friday morning Mike asked Dad if he could put his name on the table, and Dad said yes. He put his name and age on the side of the table, and Mom and Dad said no one would believe that he was thirteen years old. He said, "Well, it is the truth," and added the city we were from.

Right after lunch, we heard loud key sounds right outside our door. The door opened, and we were ready to go. They gave back our few belongings, and we all got on a bus with other people from the same jail. We were the only Romanians. Our ride was about two to three hours long. It looked like a beautiful country. There wasn't much to do on the bus ride except reminisce about events that had happened. Mom said it hadn't been too long ago when all of us had been together, and now we were spread over three continents: John was in Canada; Augustin, Violeta and Andrea were in Australia; and she didn't know where George was. She hoped that he would be in Traiskirchen, where we were going.

Before too long the bus driver honked the horn, a man opened a gate so the bus could pass through. We drove slowly between some buildings and stopped in front of a four-story building, where we all got off the bus. Someone said it was the quarantine building. At this point we didn't know anything about what was going to happen next, so we just went along with the crowd. We all walked in and were asked to sit in the next room and wait for someone to come to talk to us. On one side of the room were beds, and on the other were chairs. We sat on the chairs and waited. It was a very large room filled with people from just about everywhere, all different countries.

After a short wait, a man came and spoke some Romanian, enough for us to understand. He asked us a lot of questions. He said we would be given a place to stay. First we had to get some toiletries and bedding to which we were assigned. We got to the next room and gave them a paper, and they said because there were so many of us, we would need a wagon to get our supplies all at once. We were shown down the hall to a smaller building.

As we looked for the proper place, we saw George walking on one of the pathways. Mom was especially happy to see him because we had had no idea where he was. He didn't come with us immediately because he was going to an appointment. He said he would come back as soon as he was finished.

We got our wagon and were told a room number, given a key, and shown a building on the other side of the property. As we walked on the pathway, we saw many different buildings, each one with a different purpose. Our place was just a small room, and we had just begun to get settled in when people began walking through as if we were not even there.

Then a man knocked on the door and introduced himself as Adam. He lived downstairs with his family and helped us settle in. He told us a little about the place, what we could do, and what we could expect from them. We didn't like the fact that people were passing through our room to get to theirs, but Adam said there was one other vacant room a few doors down. He left for a few minutes, and a woman by the name of Brenda came and invited us to have dinner at her apartment. We found out later she was Adam's wife. As we were getting to know each other's families, George was looking for us. We went back to our room and sat and talked for a long time. We had been through a long day, but at the same time it was good to see George and just be by ourselves.

The next day we moved to the empty place down the hallway where no one could walk through. It was a lot better. We had plenty of beds, and it was much nicer for our family.

In the coming few days, we had to fill out a lot of forms. We got to meet all the people who lived in that building and all around us. We made friends and even went out to buy stamps and wrote letters to everyone, letting them know where we were.

Traiskirchen was a small town that had a lot of personality. The weather was warming up little by little, and we were able to go out and see the towns around us. Every so often, we had to go to the office, which was in the same courtyard as our building. A few weeks later, we got temporary work permits for the grown-ups, which included Mom, Dad, Lena, and Sandy, although it was very hard to get a job because we had no transportation and did not speak German. Dad was a lucky man—he got a job working in construction with George and a group of younger men who spoke some German. The employer even provided transportation to the job site.

In April, we got some good news that we had been given an appointment with the American Embassy. We were all excited and wanted everything to go perfectly. We told everyone our good news. Brenda and some others who had been there said that if the embassy staff said okay at the end of the interview, we had a good chance of being accepted. In the meantime, we were sent for medical examinations, which we thought went well.

In June we were told that the American Embassy had accepted us. We were happy to hear some good news finally. However, we were asked if we had any family or friends who lived in America. We didn't. The office people said that in that case, they would look for a church that could sponsor us. They sent our information to a lot of churches in different parts of the country. Then our job was to wait and be patient. Dad had his job, and so did George.

The people in the refugee camp were mostly men; there weren't too many women or families, but there were a few. We met most of those people at church, and each Sunday, people talked about when and where they were going. It seemed that most single people and small families were sponsored very quickly and that their wait was about ten weeks or so. It was still June and our time had come, but no one wanted to take on such a large family. There were ten of us: eight kids and two parents. At one point, they suggested splitting our family up, but that was not an option for us. At the church on Sundays, Dad asked people who were ready to go to talk to church members once they were in the United States so maybe someone would sponsor us. Mom told Dad not to believe in people, because people don't move people, God moves people, and because God had brought us this far, he was not going to leave us halfway on our journey. "When you depend on people the most, they will let you down. That's when you go before God," Mom would tell Dad.

While we waited, we took advantage of the time and walked as far as Baden, which was about four miles away, to see the beautiful countryside. A few times we took the train to Vienna, which was about twenty miles from where we were. Little by little we kids learned a bit of the German language, which at the time was helpful. We didn't attend school because we didn't know when we were leaving. It was getting to be very frustrating every time some of our friends left and we still had to wait. A lot of people who had arrived after us left before us. But we were happy for them, because we knew our turn would come soon.

It got to be August, and most of the people we knew were gone and new people were getting ready to go. We couldn't help feeling bad because no one wanted to have us. Once again we watched the world go by and felt we were left out. Brenda and Adam were constantly reassuring us that soon enough we would go, too.

Brenda and her family had been in Traiskirchen for more than a year, but they were going to stay in Austria, so their paperwork was going differently from ours. At the main building was a billboard with all kinds of lists, including mail. If you had mail, you could pick it up only at a certain time of the day, and if you had an appointment, the time and where you needed to be was listed. No one looked for you and reminded you, but that was never a problem because we all looked at those boards every day. A new list came up every day at 4:00 p.m. All our paperwork and passports were complete, so we looked at the board every day, hoping our name would be there.

September came with still no word of us
leaving. Once in a great while people would be
called to the office on the intercom. On September
2, they called our name, but none of us heard it,
so on September 3 or 4 they sent a messenger to
tell us to go to the office immediately. Mom and
Dad went right away and discovered that we were
going to New York on September 12. We were
announced in a very unusual way, because our
name was not on the list. That same evening we
were sitting out on the front lawn, visiting with
a lot of other people, when two boys came over.
We knew them but not that well, and one of them
asked if we were the Dejeu family. We said yes.
He said, "Oh, you are going to New York on the
twelfth." Mom asked him how he knew, and he
said he had seen our name on the board. Mike

and Zoe went to the board, and our name had been put on it. Now it was sinking in— it was official—we were going. We didn't have much notice, and Mom bought us new outfits for the trip. We wanted to have a small party the night before, and Mom said yes, just keep it small. We agreed.

On September 11 we took back all the blankets and other things that had been given to us when we first arrived. By noon that day, we had to take our luggage to be checked in. The only things we had left were the clothes we were wearing, which we planned to leave behind, and the new clothes we had bought for the trip. We gave our last pots and hot plate to Brenda to give to whoever needed them in the future. The only other things we had were paper products for the party and snacks.

The party was supposed to start around 7:00 p.m. We didn't eat much lunch or dinner because we were so excited. We had taken a bath one by one toward evening. It was a hot day, and the heat continued through the night. People stopped by through the afternoon to say goodbye and wish us well.

Around 6:00 p.m. the people who came by ended up staying. More came, and we didn't know if there would be enough room. Before we knew it, it was late, and you could barely make it in and out because there were so many people. Everyone who knew us came. Around 9:00 p.m. or so, one by one, we took our clothes and went to Brenda's place to change. The kids were in and out, playing with their friends. It was a very nice party.

It must have been 11:00 p.m. when some people who had to work the next day began to leave. As it was getting closer to our time to go, people wished us good luck and returned to their places. Mom made sure that our clothes were changed and that we didn't get dirty. It must have been 1:00 a.m. on September 12 when we got our last small bags. We said goodbye to our small but comfortable place. We started to walk to the front gate. I think about ten to fifteen people were with us when we were finally ready to go down in front to the bus that was taking us to the airport. It was a warm night as we walked slowly to the check-in area. We continued to talk and visit with our friends, and they stayed with us until our names were called. We all got on the bus, and soon after, the bus slowly took off. The gate opened and we waved at our friends until the bus turned. We were on our way to the airport!

We stayed together, and before we knew it, we were on the plane taking off. This was our first plane ride, and it was quite amazing. I don't know how the seating arrangements went, but I sat next to a Romanian man named Anghel. We had known him for a while. I was a bit scared, but he was a funny man and kept making me laugh, so it wasn't too bad. It was 4:30 a.m. when we got on the plane, and there wasn't much to see because it was dark outside. I slept for most of the flight. After a good, long nap, the plane stopped in Quebec, Canada, to refuel. Outside it was raining hard. The attendants said we would wait about an hour or so before going on to New York.

At 9:00 a.m. we arrived in New York. We all got off and didn't know where we were going from the airport. They called our name, and we stepped off to the side, but George wasn't with us. Mom was asking about George, and some woman said his name was on a list to go to Los Angeles. There was nothing we could do because they had listed his name separately, but no one had told us. They said we were going to Washington, D.C., and walked us to a different terminal, where we would wait four hours until our plane came. Someone came and asked us to go on a tour bus through New York, and because we didn't understand what anyone was saying, we went along. From the time we got into New York at Kennedy Airport until the time we got on the plane to go to Washington, D.C., we were moved around quite a bit. From JFK we were taken to LaGuardia airport and had a little tour of the city. At the time we didn't know there was another airport.

We got off the second plane late in the day and were all pretty tired. As we disembarked, we looked around and saw two men, one of them holding a sign with our last name on it. We were hoping they could speak Romanian, but they couldn't. One of them spoke some German, and we kids knew some, so that's how we got along. After we retrieved our bags, we got into two vans and were driven to Maryland. It must have been 7:00 p.m., still on September 12, 1981. One man walked us to the fourth floor of a hotel and showed us four rooms. He told us to put our bags down and go down to eat dinner. After dinner a woman by the name of Lucy came with us, showed us around, and told us about the place, but we couldn't understand what she was saying. It was a very hot night. In the morning, Lucy and the man came and continued to show us around. There were four hotels, one next to the other. There were farms on one side. It was a very small town. The man told us he was going to look for a Romanian community where we could live.

We stayed at the hotel from September 12 to September 24. The whole time we were there, we never saw any children or any schools. The town had a small general store and the prettiest houses. Every couple of days they had tour buses with senior citizens come in at night and leave in the morning. On the night of September 24, the man came and said he had found a church in Detroit where the pastor knew Dad from many years earlier. So the next afternoon we were on our way to Detroit. We were back in the two vans headed toward the airport. We said our thanks and our goodbyes, although we couldn't understand each other very well. As we got off the plane in Detroit, we finally heard other people speaking Romanian. It was such a relief to be able to talk to somebody who really understood what we were saying.

We stayed at the house next to the church. A lot of people came to see us in the first few days. At that time we felt they were just coming to stare at us. We didn't have anything except a few clothes. Someone came and brought us some pots and pans, which came in handy. The adults were nice, but the kids were snotty and rude at times. Dad went to get our social security cards, and soon after we enrolled in school. The smaller kids had a good experience with school. Because I was older, the Romanian kids and other kids made fun of me. I told Mom I didn't want to go back to school, but she constantly reassured me that it would get better.

Detroit was cold and getting even colder, and we were not used to it. We wanted to move but didn't have much money. At the beginning, the church gave us some money. Dad tried to look for a job, but nothing came up. People who had been there for years were getting laid off from work. Dad must have told his friends from church that he wanted to move to California, because one Sunday afternoon, a man named Peter came to visit us and said he was going to go to California to see some friends. He wanted to see if we were interested in going at the same time. Lena and Sandy asked Mom if they could go. They were hoping to find George and get jobs. The word was that jobs were easier to find in California. There was some talk about how the girls could stay with a family in California until we could get out there.

By the middle of October, Lena and Sandy were gone. We got to know the town a little bit more, and it was nice but still getting colder by the day. We got a letter from California, and the girls sent a phone number. We went down to the corner store to use the pay phone to talk to them because we didn't have a phone where we were staying. We tried to call every weekend. The girls were doing well and had jobs cleaning a church. The first time they got paid, they looked for a house to rent. We kids were complaining about the cold weather in the mornings and wanted to move.

Mom and Dad didn't have much money to enable us to fly. Driving was the only choice, but Dad didn't have a car or know how to drive. One Sunday, he asked some people if anyone had a car or would be interested in going to California. A few days later, a boy by the name of Mike B. came to see us after church and said he had been laid off from his job and wanted to move to Los Angeles to his brother's house. He didn't have a car, however. Dad and Mike B. came up with an understanding that Dad would buy a car, and Mike B. would drive us to California. Then Dad would buy him a bus ticket to his brother's. The girls told us they had rented a house that would be available on December 5, 1981.

We got our papers from school. In the meantime, Dad bought the biggest car Ford had ever put on the market for two hundred dollars. On December 5 we put our very few things in the car, and on Sunday morning we started going west. We didn't stop in very many places, only to buy gas and to sleep, which we did in the car. There were eight of us, including Mike B., so the car was pretty crowded. We were in the car from Sunday morning until ten o'clock Tuesday night. The only thing we looked for while in the car was the names of the new states we passed through. The more states we passed, the closer we were to California. The happiest moment of our trip was when we saw the sign that said Welcome to California.

When we arrived in Bakersfield, we stopped at a store and bought food for a picnic. We drove to a rest area and got out of the car for the longest time since we had started our trip. We stayed for more than an hour. It was sunny and warm and just wonderful to be out of the car. We were very excited to see what our new home looked like. When we got into town, we had the address, but somehow we drove by twice before we saw a big sign Sandy, Lena, and three of their friends had made that said Welcome to California.

That's when our trip was finally over, and we were glad of it. We had real beds in which to sleep and a bathroom in which to shower. It was a great relief to be on our own without people coming up and staring at us. Sandy and Lena knew only a handful of people who were Romanian: the couple with whom they had stayed and three single men who were renting an apartment not too far from us. It was a bit hard to start back to school without a translator, but we made do. Although it was December, the weather in California was warm.

Once we were settled in, we began looking for George. In January or so, we got through to some people at a church in Los Angeles and asked them to look for him and give him our phone number. It wasn't too long before we received a phone call from George, and then he came to live with us in Hayward. Our family was coming together slowly. John was working on coming to California, and Augustin and his family were trying to come, too. We were not all together yet, but we knew where everyone was and how they were doing.

It was two years or so before we were all together. Now, years later,, most of us live on the West Coast. Most of us are married and have children of our own. Mom and Dad have twenty one grandchildren and three great grandchildren.

I hope that I never again have to go through anything like our journey from Romania, but if I do, I hope that I inherited the strength, courage, and faith that my mom showed us over the years.

Printed in the United States
By Bookmasters